My Nose

Kathy Furgang

The Rosen Publishing Group's

For Jennifer

Published in 2001 by The Rosen Publishing Group, Inc.
29 East 21st Street, New York, NY 10010

First Edition

Book Design: Kim Sonsky

Illustration Credits: All organ 3-D illustrations © Lifeart/TechPool Studios, Inc.; All other illustrations by Kim Sonsky.

Furgang, Kathy.
  My nose/by Kathy Furgang.
    p. cm.–(My body)
  Includes index.
  Summary: Explains the parts of the nose, its functions in connection with smelling and breathing, and the power and importance of the sense of smell in people and other animals.
ISBN 0-8239-5576-1 (alk. paper)
  1. Smell–Juvenile literature. 2. Nose–Juvenile literature. [1. Nose. 2. Smell. 3. Senses and sensation.] I. Title.

QP548 .F87 2000
  612.8'6–dc21   99-045240

Manufactured in the United States of America

Contents

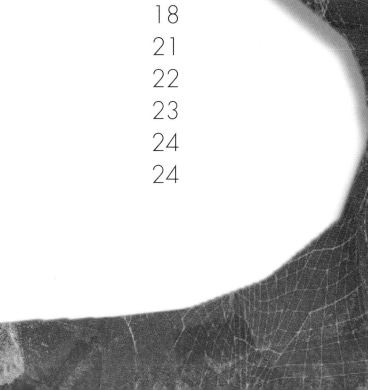

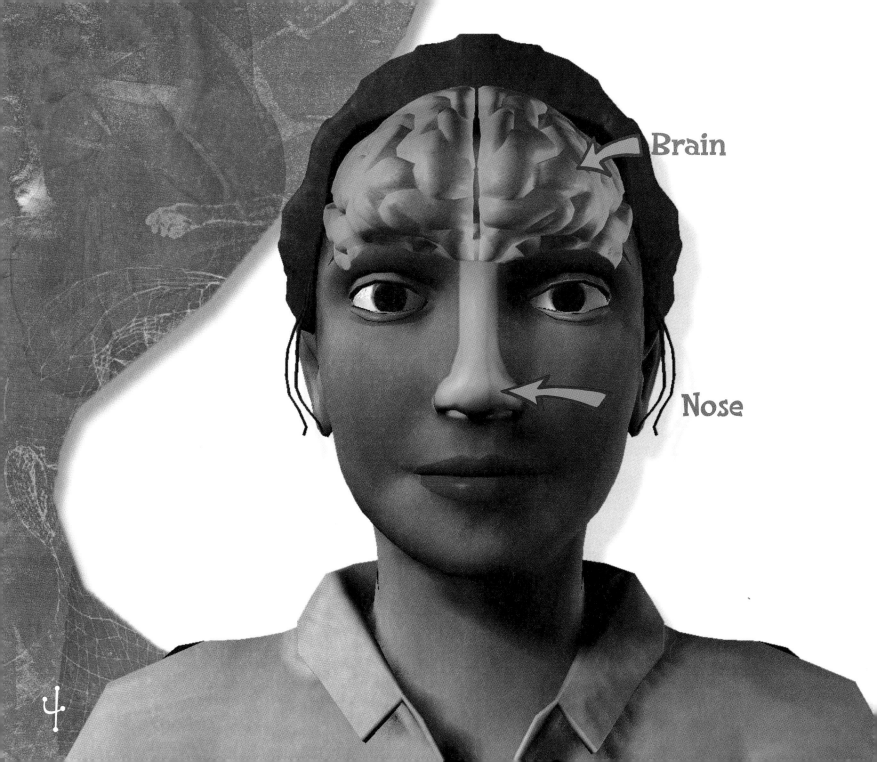

Brain

Nose

Your Nose

How can you tell that chocolate chip cookies are baking in the oven? Your nose is the body part that tells you how things smell. Your nose is a **sense organ**. Your ears, eyes, and mouth are other sense organs. A sense organ is a body part that helps your brain understand things about the world around you. Your nose sends messages to your brain about smells. Your nose also takes in air so that you can breathe.

Smell is one of our five senses. Our other senses are sight, hearing, touch, and taste. Senses tell us things about the world around us.

Parts of Your Nose

Air goes in and out of your nose so that you can breathe. Your nose has two **nostrils** that air travels through. Tiny hairs called **cilia** line the insides of both nostrils to trap dirt and prevent it from entering your nose. The space behind each nostril, inside your nose, is called a **nasal cavity**. You have two nasal cavities. As air from the nostrils moves into the nasal cavities, it hits a bundle of tiny **cells** called the **olfactory nerves**. Olfactory nerves are cells that send messages to your brain about smell. The air in your nasal cavities then travels to the back of your throat and down into your body.

Your olfactory nerves are in a patch about the size of a postage stamp. This patch has about 10 million nerve cells in it.

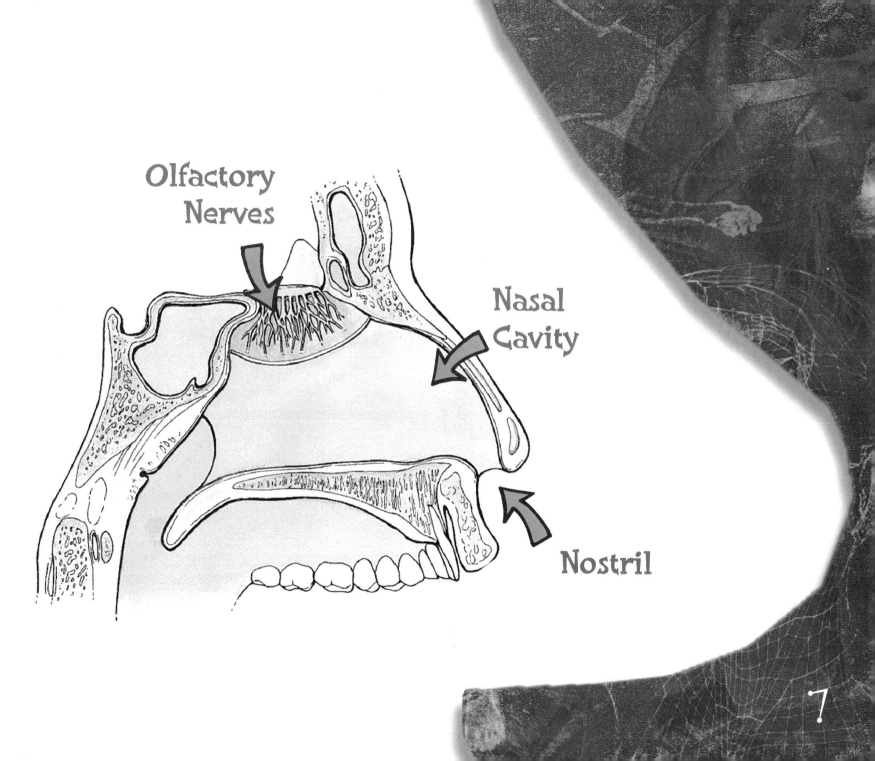

Olfactory
Nerves

Nasal
Cavity

Nostril

Smell

When you walk into the school lunchroom, you probably smell many different things. Your nose can tell that pizza, cooked spinach, and blueberry pie are being served for lunch. How can your nose tell these smells apart? It can't. It is not your nose but rather your brain that tells the scents apart. The air contains chemicals called **scent particles**. These scent particles come from everywhere. They come from flowers, food, the grass after it has been cut, animals, pollution, and much more. When you breathe scent particles into your nose, they reach your olfactory nerves. These nerves send messages to your brain. It is your brain that understands them as smells.

Does the smell of hot chocolate make you think of winter? Does the smell of flowers make you think of spring? Your sense of smell can trigger memories.

Taste

Smell is not the only sense that comes from your nose. You also need your nose for the sense of taste. Your tongue has cells called **taste buds**. These taste buds help your brain tell you what you are eating. Your nose and tongue must work together so that your brain can tell the difference between foods. Does an apple taste different from an onion? It does, but many people cannot tell these tastes apart if their eyes are closed and they hold their nose! Together the senses of smell and taste give your brain information about the foods you eat.

It is your nose and taste buds working together that tell your brain what it is tasting. If you close your eyes and hold your nose, you might not be able to tell the difference between an apple and an onion.

12

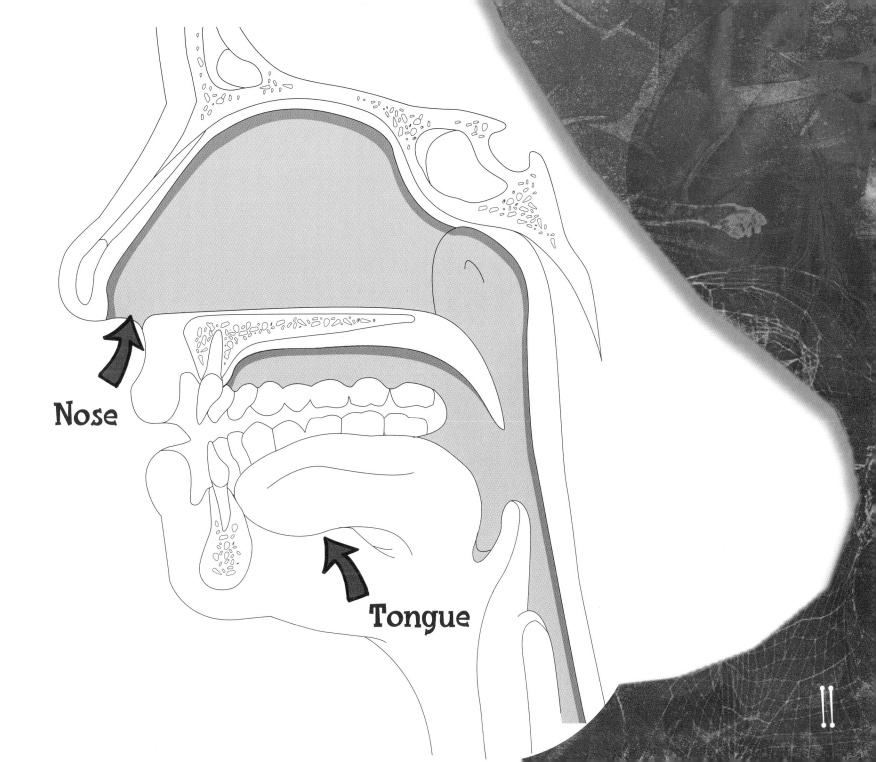

Nose

Tongue

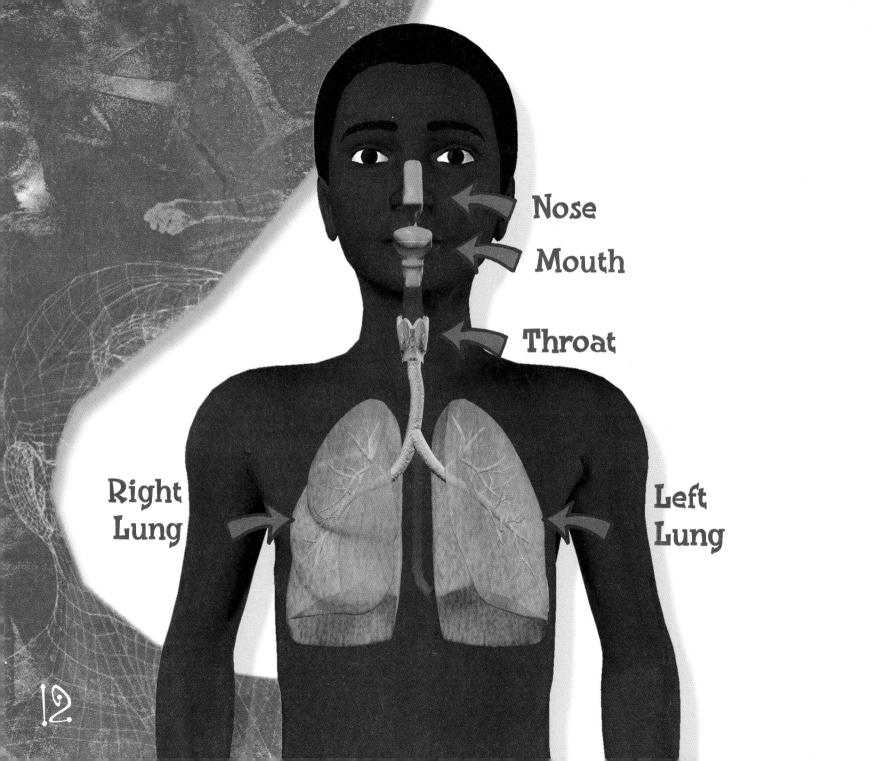

Nose

Mouth

Throat

Right
Lung

Left
Lung

12

Lungs and Breathing

   Where does air go after it enters your nose and goes into your nasal cavities? It keeps traveling down into your body. Your nasal cavities are connected to the back of your throat. You can breathe through your nose or your mouth because both are connected to your throat. All the air you breathe travels to the same place. The air travels deep into your chest and reaches your lungs. Your lungs are what allow you to breathe and stay alive. The air breathed through your mouth and your nose is basically the same. Air in your nose, however, is made warmer and moister by your body before it reaches your lungs.

When you breathe normally, air makes its way into your body and to your lungs. When you take a deep breath of air through your nose, air first reaches up to hit the tiny cells called your olfactory nerves.

The Common Cold

When you get a cold, your body works to fight it off. One way that it does this is by making a thick, sticky liquid called **mucus**. Mucus is made in your nose and throat all of the time. It is your body's way of fighting illnesses in your breathing passages. When you have a cold, your body makes a lot more mucus to help fight the illness. Too much mucus, however, will stop scent particles from reaching the olfactory nerves in your nasal cavities. That is why you often have trouble smelling when you have a cold.

It is important to keep your nasal passages clean and clear so that you can breathe and smell. Gently blowing your nose is a good way to get mucus out of your nose.

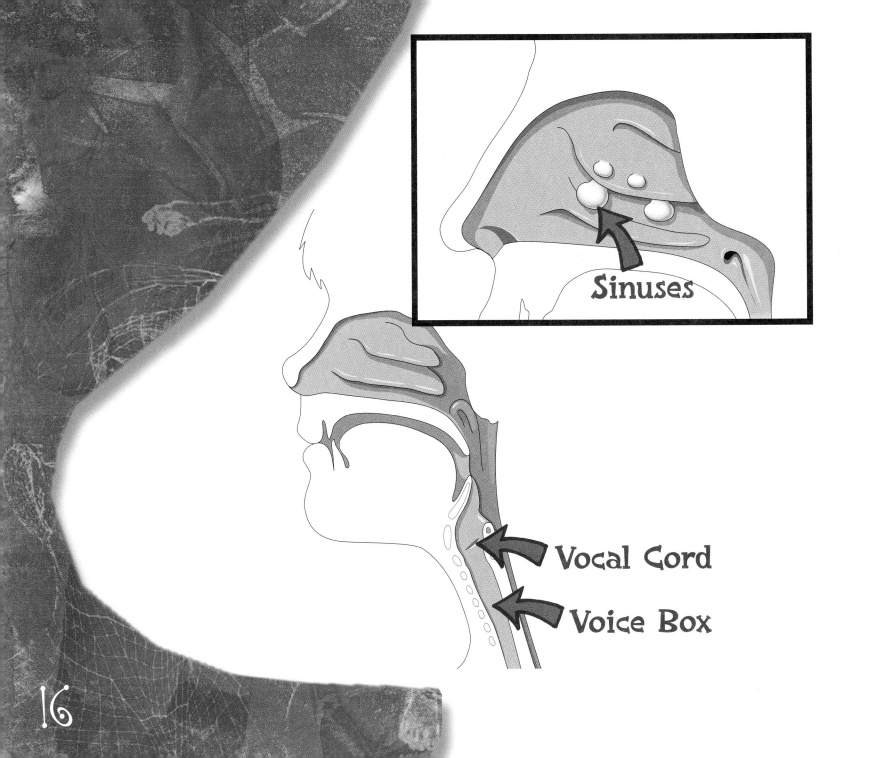

Sinuses

Vocal Cord

Voice Box

Voice

The air you breathe passes an important body part before it reaches your lungs. On its way down (and back out of) your throat, air passes by your **voice box**. Your voice box is what makes it possible for you to make sounds and speak. For you to be heard, your voice box needs air. The air traveling in and out of your throat makes the **vocal cords** around your voice box move. This helps to form sounds when you speak. Hold your nose and then talk. Your voice sounds funny because it is not able to echo through the small holes inside your head called **sinuses**. These sinuses and cheekbones are connected to your nasal cavities. They help your voice sound fuller.

 It is hard to sing with your nose plugged. Normally your voice echoes through your sinuses, which gives it a nice sound.

Sinuses

There are eight small, empty spaces around your cheekbones and your eyes called sinuses. These sinuses are connected to your nose. They help make your voice sound nice. They also make the air that you breathe in moist and warm before it reaches your lungs. Your sinuses are filled with air and are lined with mucus. When you have a cold, extra mucus builds up around your sinuses. This blocks some air from entering. Your head then begins to feel heavy because it is filled with more mucus than usual. Blocked sinuses can give you a headache.

You have sinuses in different places in your head. They are in your forehead, behind your eyes, and in your cheekbones.

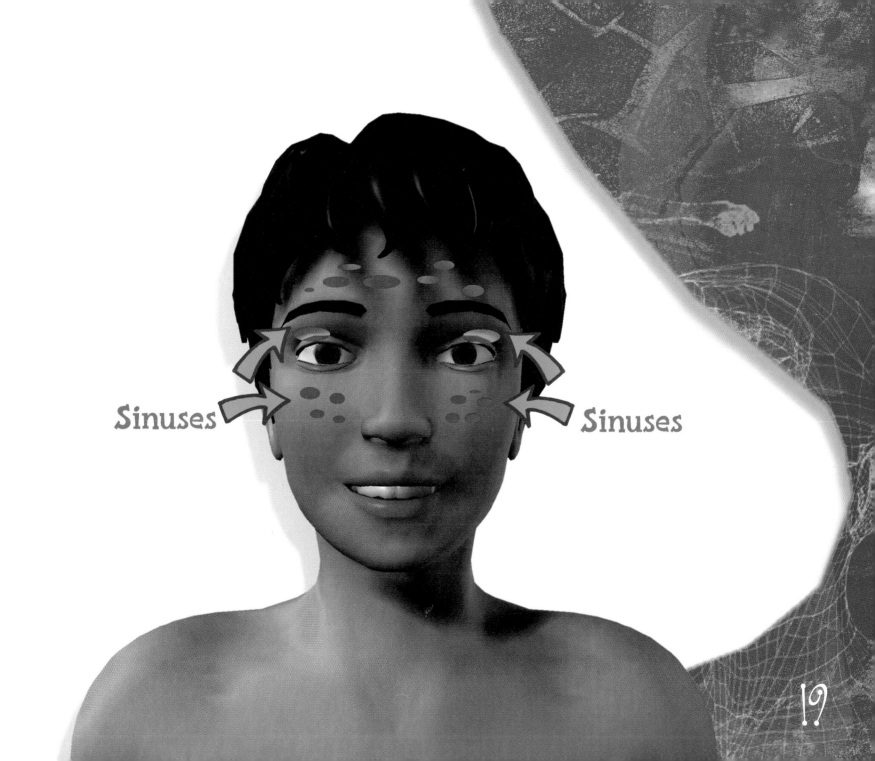

Sinuses

Sinuses

19

A Dog's Olfactory Nerves

Other Animals' Noses

Who has a better sense of smell, you or a dog? A dog's sense of smell is far better than a human's. Some dogs can follow the scent of another animal for a mile (1.6 km) or more. Since dogs have such a good sense of smell, police use them to search for drugs or to find criminals. In fact most animals can smell much better than we can. Many animals depend on their sense of smell to find food or to know when danger is near. Moles depend on their noses for information about the world around them because they can barely see at all. Snakes use their sense of smell to hunt for food. They actually use their tongues to pick up scents!

 The olfactory nerves in a dog's nose are 100 times bigger than those in your nose.

Good Smells

A person with a very good sense of smell can tell the difference between 10,000 different odors! Most people can recognize only about 4,000 different scents. Some people even have jobs in which their sense of smell is very important. Chefs and wine tasters need to have a strong sense of smell so that their sense of taste will work well. People who make and test perfumes also need a good sense of smell. Things sometimes smell differently to different people. What smells good to you may be a bad odor to someone else. Scientists say that once you learn what an odor is, such as popcorn or chocolate, you will always know it when you smell it in the future.

Glossary

cells (SELZ) Tiny units that make up all living things.

cilia (SIH-lee-ah) Tiny hairs that line both nostrils and keep dirt from entering the nose.

mucus (MEW-kus) Thick, sticky liquid made in the nose that keeps dirt and germs from entering the body.

nasal cavity (NAY-zil KAHV-ih-tee) The space behind each nostril, inside the nose.

nostrils (NAH-strulz) Two passages in the nose that help bring air in and out of the body.

olfactory nerves (ohl-FAHK-tor-ee NURVZ) A bundle of tiny cells in the nasal cavity that sends the brain messages about smell.

scent particles (SENT PARH-tih-kuhlz) Chemicals in the air that give the body clues about smell.

sense organ (SENS OR-gahn) A body part that helps your brain understand things about the world around you. Ears, eyes, nose, and mouth are sense organs.

sinuses (SY-nuh-sez) Empty spaces around the forehead, cheekbones, and eyes that are connected to the nose.

taste buds (TAYST BUDZ) Cells found in the tongue that send messages to the brain about taste.

vocal cords (VOH-kul KORDZ) Two small pieces of tissue that stretch across the voice box and move to make sounds.

voice box (VOYS BOX) The opening in the back of the throat that allows a person or animal to speak or make sounds.

Index

Web Sites

To learn more about your nose and your sense of smell, check out these Web sites:

http://tqjunior.advanced.org/3750/smell/smell.html

http://tqjunior.advanced.org/3750/taste/taste.html

24